The Fervent Crab

The Fervent Crab

Poems by Samuel Michael Wildenradt

Copyright © 2012, Samuel Michael Wildenradt

All rights reserved. No part of this book may be reproduced, stored, or transmitted by any means—whether auditory, graphic, mechanical, or electronic—without written permission of both publisher and author, except in the case of brief excerpts used in critical articles and reviews. Unauthorized reproduction of any part of this work is illegal and is punishable by law.

ISBN 978-1-4710-4939-2

I will never forgive you, nor ask you to forgive me. But in my last moment of sadness, I thank you for all the misery. This is my gift to you.

—Destruction

Contents

Child Cycle 1

A Spoiled Afternoon 2

Death as Forgotten 3

The Holy Father 4

The Prisoner Stationed Death 5

To the Literal Reader 6

Envious Youth 7

Lolla 8

The Ninny 9

Cream 10

Inanimate Objects 11

Mouthful of Mice 12

Vile Humor 13

Strumpet 14

Nasty Old Man 15

Old Hall 16

Lor 18

The Large Wall 19

My Dearest Flame 20

It Emulates the Idolatrous 21

The Rosemary 22

Londis 23

Three-tiered Cake 25

The Devil's Cherry 26

The Bluebell Giant 27

Exhibition 28

Boils 29

Great Grandfather Turnip 31

The Fallen Bear 33

Happy Birthday 35

Standing Goodwill 36

See How They Run 37

Axel 38

A Stone's Suicide Note 40

Child Cycle

The postman will die before his next delivery.
A substitute will take his place
And realize he too will die before his last shift.

The births of blue-eyed babies will flood
Over the brown-haired angels,
And their stomachs will bloat

And bother their mothers.
But nothing will change for the caged bird
Pecking at its feathers violently,

Ready to exit and become extinct.

Backyard forests
Filled with dead junkyard dogs
Will be racked and showered, unfortunately.

The pipes belonging to the broken porcelain sinks
Will wait forever to be glued back together
And all these particles of matter,

Garbage that shines in the light,
Will die and stay here to rot
Below our feet.

And it's sad… life's mosaic is sad.

A Spoiled Afternoon

The time was never like the present
And the coffee continued to mold on the stove.
As to why she cooked the coffee on the left burner,
Starring dead at its boiling over,
Is a question she did not know.

The ringing of the alarm
Confused her, as she walked to the pale-yellow door.
When she squinted her eye to look through the peephole
She found herself standing
Still at the stove.

There was no confusion—
And if there had been, it wouldn't have changed a thing.
She persisted to stand,
Molding the coffee,
While the right burner advanced its flame.

Blank—she felt nothing encompassing,
The room sat still in balance with her.
Though there was the smell of mold
Suffocating the oranges,
She stood standing, valuing their pure color.

Death as Forgotten

I will be forgotten.
Though I hold no Jewish nose.
A museum will refuse to mount my leftovers,
Microscopic signs of a dead chromosome.

The war was only told to me
By a teacher in position like mine.
I guess we will not be remembered
As siblings, but only as wasted time.

Their frames were so different,
I assume their skin was needled on.
But closer gazing of our proportions
Shows a root of descendants not quite gone.

But they are remembered
And at rest, they sleep in lines.
For those of us outside tradition,
We were forgotten in warning and wait in this everlasting line.

Promised, the Gods will not encourage change,
I have asked the one I know.
He was shepherd to both flocks of lambs
Giving no chance of repentance, he cut our throats.

The Holy Father

I have impregnated the stars.
Moon,
You do not surface my soul
Any more than the dirt
Housed beneath my nails.
So you are nothing
But a round ball of dough,
Fervent and infected yeast.
Disappear moon!
You have to go!

Ah, there it is,
My clan of victimized specks.
Alone,
And partially divorced from your master.
Nailed to a blackboard
Positioned like an iron plate
To protect your lover's chest.

Falling stars?
I know of none.
I guard the gals at night
And alternate my schedule
Whenever one's awake.
Father needs no invite.

The Prisoner Stationed Death

Inspired by the death of a loved one,
Who drove his life by an external
Appreciation for the job,
Patiently controls my cold mind of sadness.
The final day threw off his fall.

He prized the possession
That myriad men prize most,
But gave little thought to his mind's attention,
Straying from an obstructed coast

He interpreted death as his verbal oath

My mind calls to his grave,
A danger man cannot live without,
And asks him to guide it to the place
Of solution as feared by the empathetic Christian,
Whose heart is still devout.

Let loose the hold you triggered,
The point rose even
Freeing the brain.
I pray for a euphoric ending to the final chapter.
Both minds have called it a day.

To the Literal Reader

Culprit in the fields,
Slaving to raise sin into the air,
Take no last breath, traitor!
The revolutionary sword adheres.

The branches will fall under your command.
You smirk knowing that truth is pivotal
To all flesh, oh, you see!
Stop in the tracks of self-righteousness
And sanction those to accompany.

Do so character,
Your selfhood relies on the use.
Boundaries blocked by the rapid building,
Alarm the Spirit's fruits.

Envious Youth

The uterus is an empty hole,
Envied in the hearts
Of the opposite fold.

Damage has been done
To both exits producing lust.
Smell of the thin outlet

Cools to the burning touch.
One only feeds the lamb
Born every other month,

Led by the capricious man
Running to the descending cliff,
Pretending to jump.

The mistakes were barely touched!

Lolla

Playful and witty,
Knees cut up during a run through the potato patch
Her father—
Thin,
Long-legged daddy long-leg
Smiles when she smiles,
Caught in her world.

Lolla—
A rainy afternoon option?
An add on to the house,
A speckled blonde egg in rest
And driven to hatch.

Curly blossom fingers,
She is loud, obnoxious at times.
Closed eyes to those around her,
She is a gem or pearl
Born outside the mouth washed tides.

Pink-bottomed envelope,
Soft,
Not that leathery red.
No hand has ever settled upon her dwarfish figure
Because the long-legged spider
Knows the damage of routine silence
And the aftereffect it would have
When Lolla,
One arm held to her back,
Walked through the potato patch

Crying tears of her dolly.
Her existence turned moldy in a day's clearing.
May her childish glow,
Unpasteurized pink,
Hold its color.

Thank you, long-legged daddy spider.

The Ninny

Hibernate to your unit, Ninny,
No one wants to acknowledge
The presence of those awful red rubber boots.
We are in agreement then, yes?

Shush, Ninny!
You do not speak to me
As you already know there is disgust
By my peering look.

Oh studious, Ninny,
Black-locks fall from ear to ear.
What you see of yourself
Is an awkward perfection,
Mounted above an envied article of beauty,

What you've framed
As a sibling
You use as a cheap mirror.

Cream

I am a spotless lamb
Raised to shed my cream-styled wool.
I am the last in the fields,
Last to call out for a meal
And in the end,
I am a lamb raised to be killed.

So what purpose do I have
If my meat is to be eaten a few years from now?
My guts, intestines, and acorn brain
Thrown past the compost
Into a deep hole with the rest of my body.
Forgotten forever.

I am a lamb raised to be killed.

Who knows,
Maybe my teeth will be used as part of an intricate floor design?
Hand-selected and restored by an archeologist
And placed in-between pebbles collecting moss.
I am a lamb raised to be killed,
A medieval superstitious find.

Among the other million lambs
I am not rare,
But possess thoughts undefined.
I am a lamb.
A glance over your shoulder
And a life followed by those after.

I am a lamb, and that's all that I am,
Raised to be killed.

Inanimate Objects

Inanimate objects
Shapes that look like hardware
Drying on the clothesline over my head,
Chime in harmonized patterns,
Ideal for a fatigued skeleton
Shutting down his temple.

I am subjected to their intolerance
And cart around a special death.

Road signs shout:
"Beware, Death ahead!"
That way the loose screws can detour around me
And take the side streets instead.

Bypassing me,
An exposed construction of God's punishing mind,
I drag to the edge of temptation,
Inhaling and exhaling slowly
And admire all that's mine.

Their metal sense:
Polish the bolts and all is fine.
Is a disease of its own
Without vaccination.

I see no cowards beside me,
Standing in front of death's dividing line.

"Beware, Death ahead!"

Mouthful of Mice

Are you thinking of me
In my black rain boots?
Or laughing at the odd noises I make
When I smoke?
I can never tell when you are happy,
So I pretend we are lovers
In an unrestricted century,
Running energetically like feral children do
When dinner is seen from afar.

I imagine us lost in our dreams,
Free to travel within each other's minds.
You can see every part I am ashamed of
And I let you—
I'd let you—
Track over the cat scratches,
Now fading;
You don't care about the cells that split.

It's this treasure—
The circumcised pieces we'd both buried in the sand
That keeps me seated by you,
Oh, the perks in the failure to conform here.
One whole scorpion heart,
Rather than half.

This is just one fossilized image
Then the filter of my joy burns my lips.
And there I am
Sitting across from you,
Frozen.

You still do not see me,
And you never will.

Vile Humor

That salty taste that cats love, you know,
The one that soothes the nerves like a pill.
Even if it's just for a few seconds
And with one other person,
It's that taste.

You get that thrill.

If it's not at the age of eight
Then wait till you are alone
And right before your friends
Have tasted it,
Sneak off, ghostly,
And claim your throne!

You get that thrill.

When it hits your tongue,
And that left side is at a loss for words—
Break the silence and giggle softly.
My God, the hands of Eden sprout right there!
You, boy, are man
Unlike the herd of mallards
Scolding those hands.

You get that thrill.

As you know,
Cats have their catnip, nestled in dingy kitchen-sink rags,
I'm sure it's the highest quality of catnip,
Made by some decaying mother,
And not some off-brand.

Those cats get that thrill,
But can only last so long on their back.
You are God to the other baby teeth monsters,
All wishing they had the urge,
The natural spinning feeling,
Not that blue-orange pill.

Strumpet

Carefully listening to his tone
And carelessly nodding yes,
Watching his chair balance itself when he leans forward
And then resting itself when he plummets back.
He has the slightest resemblance of a man
And all the characteristics of a grazing cow.
If he only knew of the promise he had,
To feed the roasted chocolate boys,
He might be of use to the population.
But he is a man;
He is disgusting and foul.

He really knows how to spot them,
Give them the gaze and reel it in.
There's something sweet about this menu,
So indulging. He says,
"You're the most beautiful lad in all the land."

He's probably someone's father,
Or some nursing-home owner.
Either way, he's a self-made dumpster,
Scrounging for day old leftovers.
He found a bulk of it to last his lifetime.
Fresh apple cider.

Nasty Old Man

He's that old man,
The one that sits alone at the pub every night,
Drinking his pints of beer.
He's English
And speculates the actions of the occasional customer.
A scorching fire—
He wants a purebred like no other.
Don't let him fool you,
The old man still has his eyesight.

Regulars of the community
Stumble in and fondle his full head of hair.
The five fingers he's truly after
Will be his in an hour,
Once the fawn is ready to be signaled in.

Old man's a Catholic.
Come to find out, he attends mass
Every Thursday and Sunday night.
So the coins that would've been given to God
Are tossed to the fawn for its beauty,
Like an offering to the church,
And the old man gets to keep his eyesight.

Old Hall

You found me at the right time;
Darkness was filling my room,
And I watched it entice the perched birds outside
My window seal,
So they left me. and
I don't blame them.

It was like a black bag of hell
Sucking the colors of serenity off my walls
And into its mouth.
Its skin was rough and smelled
Of dead Japanese ladybugs.

To it,
I was inferior,
An indecisive toddler it could fool.
The black bag slept underneath my desk
As I studied, whining,
Then whimpering like a mule.

I feared it since the beginning,
Yet was comforted knowing I wasn't alone.
It was the devil fathering me,
I was convinced,
But this father had hooves,
Rather than toes.

For five months it had me
Locked in its black bag morning and night.
As an elementary schoolteacher once told me,
"You are not smart enough to do what's right."
And I believed her:
The devil's daughter.

That day came,
That day when water sounds so good.
I was thirsty and there it was,
My liquid solution,
The nail I couldn't swallow during my childhood.

And as I held it,
Cradling it like a stillborn baby,
I saw Old Hall with its fields of opportunity,
Inspiring a Jesuit writer
Teemed of controversy.

I saw the Bumblebee,
The insect my mother said I was since birth.
And it flew right to my eardrum,
Buzzing and pollinating my future.
I am the Genesis of a Bumblebee.

The May of traditional climbing
Brought gloom till its end.
And the lush tapestry of the Bumblebee in the wild,
Hindered my tear ducts
So I'd not be the negative.

Old Hall found me and
Wet my throat on its own.
It sacrificed its gardens
So I could touch
Its cobblestone.

The black bag shrunk
And I tried to throw it away,
But as desperate as I was to rid, myself, of it,
I am its owner
And for that, its been saved.

I flew with the Bumblebee
And sat cross-legged in front of Flatford Mill.
I walked through the heart of John Constable,
Smelling the flesh of the Dedham Vale.

Lor

She is the queen of Bohemia,
Thinner than any strand of hair on her head.
She's got pointed toes and a humor—
Some find annoying—
But her beauty is natural,
And her spirit is dead.

I am her shadow,
The reflection of his absence
Some twelve years ago.
I embody her fears, passions, and talents.
She's a Shakespearian tragedy,
Stomaching the acid

Of clear-water pond toads.
Carbon Monoxide was a family friend
She grew up with.
Short-tales of horses and canopy beds.
Boys found her attractive
And shook hands with her daddy.

She liked this.
That was their token to sleep in her bed.
Her mother,
Complicated cornstalk, signature red—
Never got over her bridge of compulsion
And died like her mama.

Lor is a virus.
I'd catch a cold from her any day.
I know she will die in the morning
That spreads itself over her body
Gracefully, and I'll bite my tongue

Till that last cord stiffens
And I know I won't stop.
Her blood will be returned to her,
As I've promised,
And I'll die with both our pains.
I know she loved me.

Lor loved me.

The Large Wall

If I could set fire to any house
Or kill a man while he sleeps,
I'd pick you—
The voice of my conscious,
The father of destruction:
You'll finally taste the fat,
You always made me eat.

That tree should have killed you
And crushed the flask that keeps you alive.
Instead, it respected my wishes
And gave me the privilege
To justly drown you.
May you feel the love I have for you
That I kept deep inside.

My Dearest Flame

You are somewhere out there crushing the solid twigs
And dried autumn leaves with your shoeless feet.
For each stone you kick out of your way into the forest,
You think of me and the distance you've traveled

For decades.
But I tell you now,
Turn back or you will die on this endless path
Trying to find me.

There's a reason as to why
Fate has challenged our meet.
You are meant to be loved by another
And I couldn't love you,
Not even if the Sun's rays dispensed unbearable heat.

Quickly turn back
Or the Gods will send a plague of rats
To crawl up your back and nibble out your eyes.
Then they will send snakes to twist around your ankles,
Making you fall, unable to get up.
I can't let them do this to you,
But if you continue searching for me,
You will die.
We will both die.

It Emulates the Idolatrous

Broken-back mermaid—
Shark tailed fin and fish lungs,
Seaweed hair, clamped open oyster earrings
Pierced into her jellyfish earlobes
Bleeding salty centipedes and worm-like discharge.
Sweet cucumber tongue
Mouthing off to the sword fish stabbing at her
Iridescent scales, wanting entry into her coral filet.

Cold red dye dripping down her
Mammoth horned chest
Attracts the one-eyed embryo seeds
As they fall out of their mother's anal coin purse
And down into the depths
Of the dark casket sea.
Small little grapes,
Born as feed to the loch under her feet.
She can only laugh as she touches her bladed coral entry

With the sea's gold key.

The Rosemary

Thirty pounds is all it costs
To sleep peacefully while it rains at night.
A goose-feather pillow and an itchy wool blanket,
Washed and dry cleaned by hand,
Mothers, the molested body,
Dipped in concrete and sand.
The broken radiator, covered with the shells
Of insects, nameless and tangled,
In one of the many spider webs,
Hums and hits the cords of
The Funeral March,
The last song that's sung to the shrinking crab.
White walls and off-white molding,
One lamp to switch on and off,
One barely opened window inviting in the mosquitoes, and
One narrow six-paneled door,
Equipped with a privacy lock.
Locked.

What walks outside the room,
Downstairs and beyond the first green door
Into the garden facing the street are men,
An assortment of tweed suites and black leather loafers,
Always walking past The Rosemary,
Turning their heads to the green door,
Wanting to marvel over their influence.
But even that door is locked,
And tonight it stays locked.
None of those men can enter in.

Londis

I jumped off the moon and flew
Downward into the sea,
Past the fairy-tailed creatures,
No one believed in, except me.
They were kind and forgave me
As I reached for their helping wings,
But they hovered over my drowning body,
Falling farther and farther
Down the deep black throat of the sea.
My vision went blind,
And my fingers numb,
And the water pushed hard on my chest,
Crushing my lungs.
My soul hadn't left me
Like my friends, now six feet above the cliff,
And the callous slab of stone grew anxious,
Anticipating its last hit.
From what I had seen earlier,
Before the jump and endless florid scene,
I thought a fall this courageous
Would rupture the two hemispheres,
Jarred in mirthless blue fluid,
Preserving oppressed memories.

I was wrong as usual.
The feeling of stupidity added pressure
To the tumor in my neck,
Bulging out and trying to free itself
And steal my last appetite:
The small glazed morsel I'd saved as a promise
To resort to if I should ever want
To resuscitate my shattered life—
And advance in the course to fight.
But I felt it gnaw its way through my skin.
And it left a crevice that would never heal,
And my thoughts died out
Like the agonizing wails of a hungry baby,
Screaming till his gums mulled around
The sugar-cane tip of his mama

And his tears can finally rest in the corner of his eyes.
I lived in a dark hole
And was pulled from it without my consent.
I am the boy who jumped off the moon
And into the sea of opportunity;
A black hole I can live in
Without the altering conditions of the seasons.
I have fallen to a death
That requires no end.

Three-tiered Cake

Latex socks,
Lined with acrylic and cashmere,
Sure to be sold at every store nationwide,
Fits the heavy midlife crisis man
Ashamed of his lisp,
And I find it attractive.
To him, I am a brother to those children,
The ones that teased him
And reappeared when he opened his eyes.
Because of this flaw,
He refuses to trust me.
So I lay in the heap of socks
He's collected over time
And I arch my back while he's behind me,
My eyes are closed
And I see him laughing.
I too, have generalized.

The Devil's Cherry

The environment around it is wild,
Its stem grows taller than any other plant.
It wants to die before it flowers.
It wants a strand of the crab's eye breath.
It wants to boil in hot water,
Then stirred with the glossy red bead.
Its attraction is fatal for children.
Its dust is rich in potency.

A pinprick won't do it justice,
And it's more than a midnight snack.
It's the precious stone jewelers are after.
It's the unlisted plant.
It's the devil's only contact.

It fears the nettles and grass snakes
Lodged deep beneath its irritated thumb.
It secretly stores its mass production
Of syrup, sweet-tasting muscle tensions,
A burning numbness on the tip of the tongue;
Its resentful indignation.

The Bluebell Giant

His ribs are hooked and hung in the cold store
Rather than chained to the tree branches
Outside next to the carports.

The rats want to gnaw through the ankle bracelet
That holds the dangling male in all his glory.
His head is missing, and the woman wonders
Where it went. His owner—
Crippled old woman who can't find a husband.
She feels sick whenever she's near his tomb

And he can't nudge her shoulder to comfort her.
Poor Bluebell. He's dinner for the commune feeders,
Rats who starve till the season is ripe.
And the blades are all sharpened,
Ready to dive into his male intestines.

Too good for the children to touch,
So they play with their thoughts of shaving him thin.
The woman has no children,
Nor the appetite to stir the spoon in the boiling stew.
She wants out of the game and nothing to do
With the fun of decorating Bluebell's grave.
"I am done," she says

And the wind blew hard
And slammed the cold store door shut.
Poor old woman.
She has no children,
But a cow named Bluebell,
Who is dead.

There is Christmas cheer because of his missing head.

Exhibition

Forty-six chromed wires were pieced together
And here I am—a whole set just for me.
What if I only want forty?
It doesn't matter what I want,
They just keep welding them together
As I break them intentionally.

I shouldn't break them,
But I do, and I make sure
Each one breaks in two.
They are so soft.
I might as well crack them,
Split them apart like a wish bone,
Throw them in opposite directions

So they can never be put back together.
Don't you dare do it!
Don't you dare destroy the joy
I've found in this grind.
And if all this was for nothing
And they survive the shattered glass pieces
That saws them apart,

Then I'll break them one last time.
They too have a mind
And they can decide what to do
Without the welder, their mother, and their father.
Now they're your enemy, and you'll hate them too.
You cannot entirely break them.

They've liberated themselves,
And they are mentally glued to you.

Boils

God, do you want to be nailed to a four-poster bed
And scrubbed clean by the bristles of my toothbrush?
Does this suit you and all your needs?
I may as well wash you in a church,
So your congregation can see
What a blind man you are, sitting there,
Hunched over like a ridiculed teen.

You don't need us.
Look me in the eyes and tell me this isn't true!
Chief of the tribe,
Leader to the golden staircase,
This is the blasphemy
You hate, is it not?
Know that the Lamb of God,

The dead sheep in the oven,
Is through with you.
Bury your face,
The mask you wear in each painting depicting 'His Majesty,'
I get sick of the ceramic crosses nailed
Above a child's bed.
It's not enough to bruise their knees
Each night before they sleep,
While they whisper the Lord's Prayer.

Like you actually listen to all these billions of
Sheep at night, fleeing to you.
Oh, merciful Father, help me!
I am but one of your miserable sheep

Straying from the herd,
Where do I go?
I know that's what you want to hear.
You want me to bow down to your gravitating feet.
As you walk on water,
I am here and here is where I'll stay.

You are the creations of a mad man,
A jester even you'd believe.

Gullible fawn, the dead sparrow
I threw a single stone at,
I send you the wrath
Of all the starving children,
The still-heart of my sea.

Kiss twice the Shepherd you persuaded
To haul me out of peaceful darkness
And into a chosen death,
Your famed disciples wrote for me.

Great Grandfather Turnip

The excitement to see you at your desk,
Holding your throbbing heart,
Stroking it like a cat,
Shakes my baby knees, intensely.
I love you.
I love it when your fingers'
Slowly trickle down my back.

I don't need to tell you where it itches,
Your psychic mind tells you it's not my chest,
But the curved dimensions behind me.
I've been given a fruit bowl back
And you're the first man
Who wants to attack.

My tiny-tear ears bless the sounds
Your chair makes as you scoot forward,
Hiding the stir inside your pants,
Crossing your legs,
I'm no idiot!
I demand to see it.
Show me the tail of the starving rat.

There is a stretch in the morning
And I plan to savor every last bit
Of the ticking clock above the kitchen sink.
So touch me, Great Grandfather Turnip,
Touch the seed that stands by your side
While she dies in a bed
Miles and miles away.

But don't think of her—
Think of me and the tension you feel
As you tiptoe down my spine.

Thank you, Great Grandfather Turnip,
You've given me the death of a flower,
One that grew by your side,
Next to the ashes of a broken spine.
I hope to see you when the air turns grey
and I fight to breath it in.

Remember my name,
Remember my flame
And tug on the tail
That sleeps limp in your grave.

The Fallen Bear

He grew out of a thought.
A daydreamer gave him
Two eyes and a narrow mouth
With lips, you'd kiss
And fall back to when the blindness
Scratched at your pupils,
And the heat rose
As the onion harvest began.
He was perfect. He followed the close line
Of our instrumental ape clan. But you
Saw the hole and tried starting over,
And you colored in the imperfections
With your favorite color—
But that was on paper—
And the man walks on land.
You went days without him,
Yet you drew more sketches
Of what he should have been
And the hole grew larger,
And then you realized,
You made this man and that hole, you hated,
Was always part of the plan.
He can't shred himself into pieces and try to conjure
An energy to scribble over your masterpiece.
Fool, you are blind and will never see!

You've outweighed the pros, and the scale
Is soon to dent and fall on your feet,
Crushing your toes, you brag about,
And you'll fall back and expect his angelic arms
To rise from the ground
And massage your inflated-sex-doll body,
Still shocked from the sight of
The stabbing Virgin Mary.

And he won't be there.
The fall will kill you,
Along with the artwork you've stored
In your mind's walk-in closet.

Years of memories
Drawn over and over,
Not one worth showing off to your friends.
But the subject you used was perfect.
The man with a hole in his chest,
Waiting for you to pencil in a heart that connects
Your X to his X.

Happy Birthday

Soft skin,
Hands that wind themselves
Up mama's totem pole fingers.
Like ivy on a barb-wired fence
The crows use as a posting spot,
Searching for the earthworms that were thrown
By the tractor clearing last month's weeds.
They are so soft and warm,
It would be easy to bend one backwards.
Too bad you can't do it,
Without waking the baby
From his vivid black dreams.
Wake up!
Please, wake up.
Tell mama if this hurts and she'll stop and let you sleep.
Take in a deep breath
And on the count of three
Squeal like a pig and let mama rock you, baby.
She'll blow mama breath on your fingers,
And you'll smile at her,
Holding in that last yelp
Behind your greedy teeth.

Standing Goodwill

Every father is different, and the sons
Belonging to these beer-battered men
Sleep in lawn chairs that overlook the golf course,
Sun shining through their licensed existence,
With no ambition to read ahead

For tomorrow's lecture
On their spatial ability
And poor reading skills,
Opposite to the girls that sit
In a row of theatre seats behind them,
Aspiring to be kindergarten teachers
Because of the nonsense their fathers said

While smoking cigars in the library.
Such an elite group of men that chew on their nails.
And as hard as they try to earn a sufficient income
So the logs continue to stack next to the stove.
Their sons will laugh at the misfortunes of others:
Boys without fathers, and the girls,
Beautiful but widowed.

The rare breed without privilege, live to defy
The grammar school pigs.
Their achievement was paid for in slander
By rich boys and their parents,
Sipping tea from a crystal wineglass.

See How They Run

Four men cried out last night.
I saw three of their bodies
Hanging from a tree in the orchard,
The next day.

Mice were climbing down the ropes they hung from.

I took a broom and swept up the empty wrappers
Of each man's death, deserved and sent to Hell.
I might have shown mercy for their sins,
If I'd been the one to follow the four that night.

But I was asleep.
I heard their crying,
And then there was silence.
This is a reasonable alibi.

The fourth man, however,
Was seen buying rope the day before
Those three barnyard hens were plucked and hung to dry.
He had to have flown over my house, sometime after midnight.

I'm always in bed before that time.
It doesn't do any good to dwell over something
So mysterious. Many men vanish to create new lives
In countries I'd like to see.

He could have used one of the dead man's passports
And sailed to Siberia or the Canary Islands.
Either destination would satisfy a man's reason to flee.
No, I don't think they'll ever find the fourth man.

The newspapers headlines read:
"Three Blind Mice Hung on String"
I laughed at this as I sipped my coffee
And spoke to a good friend
Inviting me to travel with him,
Somewhere overseas.

Axel

Shrinking to almost nothing desirable,
Pale, thin, and conscious of fate,
There is little worry over the serving portions
The nieces and nephews will fight over this Thanksgiving.
But his deteriorating attention to detail
Magnifies heavily on his children
And their self-promotions of threatening mistakes.

A lineage of wild rats,
Tall with an assortment of likes,
Were shown the same beating love their father
Feared as a child.
He grew a passionate fist
That shined like the blade of a knife.

"Honor thy father," he said,
When a rat spoke out of turn
And the bigger rats entertained themselves
With matches and the celluloid doll their sister loved,
And would never get returned.

So as all the rats grew older,
And their nails grew sharp. Unable to feel pain,
Their father held his fist to each of their faces
And threatened them with a beating,
But their eyes were already bloodshot with some
Other hit that had stood in line,

Next to their father for years,
Sprinkling a chemical that hollows out the heart
And chiseled the brain.
Sifting over their heads like the first day
Of snow: December runs through their veins.
And he lost them in a one-bedroom house
He claims he built by his own two hands.

His sons tell the same story
When he's not listening.
And the truth is,
They are all sewer rats

Chasing after their own tails
And experimenting with death and a canine toothache.

He has a few months left to count the beats
Of his repositioned heart
And he's accepted the train ride to heaven
And the chance of a delay.

A Stone's Suicide Note

Warm, volcanic waters immerge from the pit
Of hidden springs and fresh blown air
In a coat pocket drowning to reach the bottom
Of the catfish migration
Circling around its moth-colored presence.
Trenches, ready for battle,
Open their sunroofs and the crystal chandeliers
Chime as the waters pull forward and break.
The ground begins to rise and platforms stretch into narrow
Sidewalks and hover over the caves and animal bones;
Museum-quality rabbit furs,
Asleep under the graveyard of whales,
Covered the marbles that hung like portraits
On a walking-stick man who slept outside
Until the Earth shook and launched a chilled reading of truth,
The book of knowledge every young man should know.

It all sinks to the bottom or aspires to do so
When time stops and the heart
Twitches at every insect noise;
Bed bugs are exempt and die within two days
Of the relaxing lavender oil a small woman insists
Would kill her, if assisted.
All we want is an escape, a map
That's drawn out and ready to fold and hide
In a secret compartment that will one day
Be found after an apocalypse covers our graves,
And what nature provides us is swept into the pit.
And every previous century is up for grabs,
Letting the minnows swim to their glorious destination,
For they are deserving of the life they've picked.

Made in the USA
Lexington, KY
14 March 2012